To George's
Karin

Счастье, здоровья,
радость.

Happiness, health,
fulfillment
Love, Elaine!

a fight to the finish

a fight to
the finish

elaine podovinikoff

VANTAGE PRESS
New York

FIRST EDITION

Published by Vantage Press, Inc.
516 West 34th Street, New York, New York 10001

Manufactured in the United States of America
ISBN: 0-533-12424-7

Library of Congress Catalog Card No.: 97-90556

0 9 8 7 6 5 4 3 2 1

Words

roll off
your tongue
your pen
your typing finger

Words

fill up
the mouth
the page
the air they linger

Words

connect
cut off
collect
crunch up and crinkle

If only we could choose
some words through time
That unite us all
and all us define . . .

Contents

Foreword   xi
Preface   xiii
Note to Readers   xv

The Agony and the Ecstasy . . .
The Whole Truth   3
Emotions   4
Happiness   4
Id-entity   5
in the bathtub   5
love   6
Love . . .   7
Music   8
the meaning of love   9
Eyes   10
Free Space   10
"That's Life!"   11
Song   12
Exit   12
identification   13
To Pete   14
Visiting Hours   15
Existence   16
On the Road   17
The Quintessential Traveller   18
Real Life   19
Help!   20
death   21
Evanescent Hope   22
lethargic lapse   23
one by one   24
deluge   25
fun amongst the ruins   26
Loneliness\Aloneness   27
Passion?   28
loneliness   29
Pursuit of Meaning—1   30

Pursuit of Meaning—2   30
Pursuit of Meaning—3   31

Of Nature and People
An Ode to Nature   35
Grand Canyon   36
Forest Primeval   37
The Highway   38
My tree   38
The Last Sacrifice   39
American Promontory   39
Ninth Wave   40
Surreal Imprint   40
Rebirth   41
Sand Shadows on a Heat-Drenched Beach   42
To My Brother   43
my first communion   44
Cottonwood Treasurehouse   45
a fight to the finish   46
ferry watch   49
sisters   50
Character   51
The Eyes Have It   52
Perception   53
Gossip   53
A Metaphor   54
Crosswinds of Character   56
To My Daughter Sarah   57
The Meaning of Being a Mom   58
An Ode to Us   59
to dad   60
Eulogy to Eileen   62
My Parents   64
To My Mother   66
Interesting . . .   67

The Quantum Quest
Folly   71
Options or Not, That Is the Question   72
What was it Shakespeare said . . .   73

being used 73
last moments in great-grandmother's life 74
On Death 75
Western Philosophy I 76
Western Philosophy II 78
apathy 80
the collector 81
Our Daily Life 82
A Mother's Daily Life 83
Respiratory System 84
Horse's Goals 85
Sometime 86
The Muse 87
The Youth of Old Age 88
lying on a beach in Venezuela, reading a magazine, while
    local poor people circle around us basking foreigners 89
Nostalgia 90
I Wish 92
I NEED 92
The Think-and-Do Book 93

Doggerel Et Al

The Recipe for Letting Your Imagination Run Away with You 97
biding our time 98
Battlecry of Our People 99
Fun with Physiognomy 100
Coffee 101
Camping 102
The Joy of Travelling 103
Stagnant Doggerel\Failing Old Guard 104
Sillification 105
Rhyming Couplets for a Rhyming Couple 106
Epilogue 107
Afterword 109

Foreword

"... and then it becomes the most frustrating thing to be confined to expressing ourselves in words and not in photographs of the true guts of thoughts. As the sounds leave the mouth, they form impressions for listeners according to the listeners' own mix of experience with those sounds, leaving each utterance to be interpreted differently. Putting the sounds on paper with strokes and curves, gives the writer an opportunity to reread the combination of words and reassess if they still reflect the thoughts she wanted to express, before sending them out into the world-at-large. Always, the marks on paper, no matter how eloquently put together, remain a feeble attempt at true communication. . . .

".... when she converted her history into words, it changed in front of her eyes, like a growth of its own with its own true history outside of her ... like the words, that in her were hers alone, yet when pushed outside of her and looking back into her eyes, became owners of their definition. . . . "

(Excerpts from *a fight to the finish,* the story.)

Preface

Doukhoborism is a highly evolved life concept that originated in Russia hundreds of years ago and places the responsibility for the future welfare of humankind squarely on the shoulders of its people. Its central tenets are based on living according to one's ever-evolving conscience and maintaining a simple life of toiling and cooperating, always close to the land. Being thus in harmony with nature would bring us in tune with God's spirit which Doukhobors believe is in each living creature, and leads to a possible heaven on earth.

This life concept was a great burden of comprehension for me when I was little and I raced away to university as fast as I could. Little did I know that the philosophy and literature that I would study and love, would land me right back at Doukhoborism's door. In fact, I remember taking a course in Shakespeare with a Jewish professor whose interpretations had a distinctly Jewish flavour. I nearly wrote my term paper on "Shakespeare Was a Doukhobor" because I found so many precious lines of verse whose inspirational meaning could have been understood by our illiterate ancestors who handed down their legacy in action, not words. They lived simply in their villages, worked hard, and answered to the dictates of their consciences. They were "true to themselves."

Now we are left cherishing the same evolved understandings in our mind, heart, and soul, but our daily life is slipping away into the capitalistic, individualistic competitive stream. It's like holding onto the corner of a blanket that's being tugged and twisted and pulled away. You could grit your teeth and rivet your eyes shut, hold on till your veins pop out blue, but the grip keeps slipping anyway.

Hypocrisy has become our daily bread, and it's killing us. We need to change our lifestyle or change our comprehensions of the universal truths we hold dear. . . . I hope we change our lifestyle, for ALL our children's sake . . . and until then, I'll keep "twirling in a whirlwind of flirting words, chasing syllables with fingers trembling of desire. I'll keep gulping down each hand's elusive grasp and living on the echoes of our history's wisdom sired."

Note to Readers

"they" say we must separate the wheat from the chaff and
throw away the chaff
it is "worthless stuff"
chaff
but we may define wheat exactly because of chaff's existence
functional deviance
the purpose of chaff

there is both wheat and chaff in these pages
the separating
is left to you

a fight to
the finish

The Agony
and
the Ecstasy . . .

a blighted day ended
stained face can't be hidden
baseness besotten
naïveté ridden

    a naked day started
    fresh face to be written
    an innocence gotten
    new juicy time bitten

The Whole Truth

To catch a glimpse of one's true unspoiled self
    in a breath of magic pooled reflection
Is to be kissed by God
       to be given a gift from Eternity
       to receive The Whole

It is this fleeting insight touch
    this mystical mistletoe connection
       free from the everyday refracted rays that
       ceaselessly bounce rebound contort distort
       multiply and crash into a waste of fragments

It is this fervent need to see
    and feel and smell again
       the total Rhyme the Tune Combined
    that makes me move ahead again in Time
    to see and feel and smell once more
    the then and now
    and evermore
    forever Truth
    that's mine!

Emotions

red green yellow
autumn leaves blowing
scattering into summer blue

black clouds hovering
ever hovering

Happiness

a little bit of blue
a little bit of green
and we make
the prettiest color
ever seen

happiness is—
aquamarine!

Id-entity

there is a road
within my mind
that winds and curves
I cannot find
the end
the final stand

there is a road
within my mind
I ride alone
and bid it stay
paved
always mine

in the bathtub

immersed
hot burning
slowly diluting

baptized once more

love

foaming visions
crowning glory
surface
above mediocrity
forever rebirth
inside
a womb of terror
love never
ends
despite agony
of days and nights
forever black
and blue
with reality
of me and you
love never ends
the candle
intense
burns anew
a thread
to fair weather
love never ends
a medical cure
a raven's feather
shaman
thank you
for eternal
forever
nature's never
extinct
however the measure
of few
and the fewer
who continue

to bloom
together
we must ever
relinquish
the heaven
thank you
for the view
thank you

Love . . .

smolders beneath the surface
erupts at sunrise
thunders through the day
mellows with nightfall
melts into dusk

Love . . .
rises and sets
forever

Music

feeding the heart
this hour
licking the soul
with power
sending the mind
a shower
of flowers
this, music does for me

working the pain
intently
lifting the weight
so gently
sending the mind
to its knees
with its breeze
this, music does to me

beating its rhythm
with clear stroke
filling the chasm
with new hope
sending the mind
to fresh places
and graces
this, music is to me

8

the meaning of love

love costs
nothing
to learn
injects
energy
to burn
love's cost is
priceless
in worth
recommended
from birth
to each
living soul
to experience
endure

love
the only pure
still
pure
trustworthy tool
human
cruel
in its worth
full
to emptying
still
love costs
nothing to learn
but
your life

Eyes

Dyes of light
Flickers of eternity
Images
Pierce the intent
Flooding left and right.

I am drowned in the sight.

Free Space

This time it's for me
This time it's just I
   No more
    for him
     for her
      for them
       for someone else's rhyme
This time it's just me
This time here at three
   It's time
    for free
     for me!

"That's Life!"

once, once just or twice
if your 7's roll in
if your Fate's calling "Gin!"

once, once maybe twice
as your calendars fly
you catch Truth in your eye

it was once, and now twice
that I happened to see
doors swung open for me
and the light seared my soul
and I fell with the blow

it's not fair, I proclaim
'cause the Truth's where we aim
yet we touch it ourselves
if we're lucky, I guess
once
once or twice

Song

Sprinkles stardust on your soul
Ethereal wings begin to grow
Words are carried to the sky
As the music makes you fly
Hopes are kindled
Bridges built
Senses heightened
Holes are filled
Sounds of music can inspire
Can revive the smouldering fire
Song

Exit

She fell into her voice
Dropped down inside the chatter
Lost in her reply

Sound gave her no choice
Muffled in the utter
Silenced by her sigh

She fell into her voice
Was swallowed by the echo
Mute inside her cry

identification

bouncing
rebounding
refracted sight

an internet
of mistaken identity
entity
representation of
mystery
confirmation
reflected
inside trading
of lifeworks

there goes
the final pattern

configuration
information
accumulated data

it doesn't matter

To Pete

comedy and tragedy
masques
for life
behind
the plastic
castes

deal the hand
and
pay the price
don
the mask
and
laugh or cry

underneath
is
buried deep
peel
a peel
and still
unchanged

comedy and tragedy
they
play their game
the
same

by birth
the mould's
been laid
there is
no
trade

laugh or cry
the dice
are
fatal

fate

Visiting Hours

Hairless
Embryonic vision of painfulness
Baptized in spiritual rebirth
Before death
After life
Filling with Truth
Everlasting strength curled
in emaciated form
Reaching beyond sightlessness
helpless immobility
to connect to the final depth
of eternal consciousness
Living soul forever
open
A blessed moment
given
in suffering

Existence

Backhanded glance
Across
The southside
Of the days

Backhanded swipe
Across
The southside
Of the face

Wiping clean
The truth
Of learning
To cope
With the reality
Of lies

On the Road

Freeways passing on each side
Cars are standing close beside
Eyes with eyes are linked in time
And the music makes its rhyme.

There is rhythm on the road
Lights and wheels and each their load
—Flash of flesh and metal grate—
In one second it's too late!

Hands are welded to the wheel
Back is arched in solid steel
Eyes are staring straight ahead
Who'd have guessed that he'd be dead.

Fellow traveller, where'd you go?
Was it your time and did you know?
Was that mutt shot straight from Hell?
To grotesquely kick Death's bell?

Freeways passing on each side
Cars are standing close beside
Eyes with eyes are linked in horror
Linked in pain and common sorrow.

The Quintessential Traveller

I'm one of those people
Who hates closing the day
Doors shutting for rest-time
Ending each holiday

I'm one of those people
Who longs for what's gone
What's coming, what's altered
The repeat of a song

I'm one of those people
Who has blessings galore
Yet looks to horizons
For what's left in store

I'm one of those people
What's there left to say?
Who loves the edge better
Than safe centre to stay

One p.s. addendum
I must add to date
I hate ending my verses
In case each seals my fate

Real Life

Another deadly axe has fallen
Echoes hollow in my head
Another ideal sliced and spoiled
Lies discarded bloodstained red.

Basest instinct pushes forward
Cutting innocence at the door
Brutal toughness throws Truth's wisdom
Like some garbage to the floor.

Foaming ego feeds the blotter
Of each body to its core
Soaked and soggy sluggish bloated
Drowns the Spirit evermore.

And I stand deaf dumb and blinded
Red blood tears squeeze from each pore
Rasping sobs grate at my insides
—Yet I still them like before.

Help!

There is a voice
that screams so loud
yet no one hears
just me
it bursts my ears
it breaks my heart
yet no one feels
like me

where is that supposed-to-be constant supply of clean quiet
thoughts that I can quickly gulp down from the
supposed-to-be forever-full oxygen tank of humanity?

I cannot breathe
I cannot think
yet no one's here
but me
I'm drowning in
a screaming rink
that blurs my eyes
to see
     at least
       me.

death

energy to dust
each
a measure of time
to the test
stillness overcomes
its final crest

life and death
each
a worth of time
to the test
consciousness freed
the last dance is best

time is at rest

Evanescent Hope

There'll be a time
I mutely said
to someone
on earth
in the din overhead

There'll come a time
in life's full span
when the echo
of sound
from the best-laid plan

Would be heard at last
And convert the pain
to laughter
and love
then peace would reign

A cruel joke it may be
To think that man
could be born
again
to understand

The cards are dealt
The time is drawn
yet howling
the life
spins on and on

Can it yet come to pass
That we'll find the place
where to sigh
and turn
to a human face?

lethargic lapse

as she sinks into the luxurious divan
in the room
designed to her particular perfections
she sighs through the huge bay window
staring deep within herself
at the deserted garden
lined with life-giving trees
green pines in the middle of winter
on a white blanket of nothingness
her mind her soul
faint flickering sunlight through pineneedles
today
only today
to see
clearly
please
once more clearly

one by one

each
drop
in
the
bucket

each
grain
of
the
sand

reflects lingering fingers of light
enhancing dances of night
caressing the heavens for flight

each
coin
in
the
pocket

each
piece
of
the
land

echoes within constant direction
forming perfect connection
purifying our instant affection

each
life
in
the
world

a priceless insight

deluge

collecting despair in a bucket
drop
        by despondent
                drop
suddenly
NIMBOSTRATUS
a torrential outpour
hopelessness
            raining and
                    draining
grey desolation
despotic despair
flooding
        drowning
                despair

fun amongst the ruins

there's sundries mondays birthdays
who cares whatdays
immaculate conceptions in threes
christ the father the son the holy ghost
it's the most
weight to freight
on two feet
let's forget the albatross
the state
of where and who and why we are
trilogies in space
the stars
are aligned to the bar
let's mars it to the end
of the lent
since it's meant
to extend us thus far
the speed is worth
the stay
that's all there is to say

Loneliness\Aloneness

Loneliness is when you need an ear
and it's missing.
Aloneness is when you have both ears
and it's quiet.

Loneliness is when there's a hole in your heart
and you can't fill it.
Aloneness is when your heart is whole.

Loneliness is longing for something.
Aloneness is longing for nothing.

Loneliness can happen in a crowd.
Aloneness thrives in solitude.

Loneliness makes you weak.
Aloneness can make you strong.

Loneliness leads to distorted thinking.
Aloneness can clarify thinking.

Loneliness divides from a lack of connection.
Aloneness divides from not needing a connection.

Loneliness makes you think of writing.
Aloneness gives you time for writing.

You can choose to be alone.
Loneliness moves in unbidden.

Too much loneliness leads to despair.
Too much aloneness leads to isolation.

Passion?

dancin'
    'tween the chasms

singin'
    'twixt the hollows

writin'
    'midst the spaces

holding onto
    vibrant
        nothingness

loneliness

there is an emptiness
a void to avoid
without a friend

there is a wretchedness
a pain to explain
without a friend

    so I walk around
    to the hollow sound
    of my heartbeat echo
    and I try to find
    some new tie that could bind
    me to peace forever
    but I hear through it all
    a far-distant call
    of my soul crying lonely
    and I feel such despair
    for there's nobody there
    to help ease the torment

there is an emptiness
a void to avoid
without a friend

there is a wretchedness
a pain to explain
without a friend

Pursuit of Meaning—1

I look
Into
Pools of light

And sink
Into
Depths of sight

Yet hold
Onto
Nothing but night

Pursuit of Meaning—2

There is truth
There are lies
There are grey
Shades of dyes
In our little white lives

There's the road
There's no end
There's a loss
In the bend
Of our fate to attend

Pursuit of Meaning—3

Invisible groping inside the vortex
Frustrated desperation piecing together
Thread by fragile thread

A glimpse of light in this fleeting smile
A spot of heat from that vanishing touch
A tiny wisp of the last conversation

Piecing together
Thread by fragile thread

Our days
Into meaning
Something

Of Nature
and
People

An Ode to Nature

O Saviour
Our Saviour
Light was thy spring
O Saviour
Our Saviour
Thy heart's in a ring

Trunks through the ages carried thy will
Now hollow treasures reserved standing still

O Saviour
Our Saviour
Hast thou lost thy voice
O Saviour
Our Saviour
Hast thou still some choice

Green had mutations echoing round
Now dusty symbols diffused barren brown

O Saviour
Our Saviour
Thou CANST raise thy sound
O Saviour
Our Saviour
Thou MUST stand thy ground

—from the people—

Grand Canyon

Silent standing
In action
Reflections of deep
Connection
Nature's pure breed
Earthly tent tops
Tu-tu twirls
Carved jade ribbon
Crewcut furrows

Hollows and swallows
Windful and sky
Mussels and burls
Lobster red dry
Cracked and cracking
Monuments spread
Nothing to follow
Nothing is led
Shadows and sunlight
Dunes of grit
Grave cliff mirrors
Rock gnarled and bit

Horizontal combing
Christened in time
Silence that's golden
With orange and blue rhyme

God's cathedrals
Etched deep in a tray
Natural history
Faint echoes away

Pray for our master
Breathe for the free
Listen to still songs
Tangible eternity

Forest Primeval

Evergreen gauntlets
probing to space
Atlases
holding the sky
in its place.

Extensions of Earth
umbilical cords
Silent
connectors to Heaven
our life-giving Lords.

The Highway

On a narrow strip
of technology—
our train.

On a fragile grip
of suspension—
our vein.

On either side—
naked nature
retained
contained
constrained.

On a finite trip
of connection—
we reign.

My tree

Proudly planted
Verdant arms straining
Full
Ready
Handing
Nature back to me

The Last Sacrifice

Succumbed tortured bones
of everything green
stretched out toward Heaven

Testimonial stripped monuments
to crucified Nature.
. . . with no Second Coming.

American Promontory

Trees
Pouring
Out of the
Contours
Of the
Craggy
Countenance
Held together
By my window

Ninth Wave

No second thoughts
No turning back
No time to wait
It is now too late

The wave is pushed
Propelled compelled
It spills distills
It disappears

Eternally

Surreal Imprint

Churlish fingernail pods
   black bulges
   suspended against
    the incandescent sky
Grotesque extremities
   on scrawny conduits
Spindly stems
   ejected out of
   chlorophylled
    lace and brush
And the gutteral
   crow ensemble
   monotonously mocking
Steaming
   the saturated air

Rebirth

The answer to no hope
Is the brink of the ocean
Overflowing with possibilities

Beyond that last wave
Is something newborne
Launched pure and fresh

Ready to spill into view

Until there is no brink to the ocean
There can be no end to hope

Sand Shadows on a Heat-Drenched Beach

Shallow one-sided graves
    of the heels
Resound with lop-sided echoes
    of a sunny day
Memorial soft hills
    of the toes
Exude evaporating memories
    of this yesterday

I lie in the fading shades
    of the clock
Tracing abandoned silhouettes
    of a bottom line
Representing the feet
    of tomorrow
Marking steps in the sand
    of their time

To My Brother
(*In Honour of Fifty Years*)

Once upon that long-ago time of our youth
we lived in a house with a sunny neighbourhood
we scaled those mountains that still blossom in spring
and cooled in the river that's outlined in green
We formed promising clubs and built unparalleled forts
planning our futures with each innocent board
ideals and visions constructing the day
when that future of ours would take us away

One short step and now fifty years have gone by
that golden season's slipped away in a sigh
we have barely begun when half of it's done
and we're looking behind and ahead for the sun
It's too late or too early or neither is right
it's that middle ground desert through which we must fight
to get to our future again is the plan .
we've yet worlds to conquer and the present's at hand

A present that's full of what fifty years brings
a family, a home, and still blossoms in spring
through the love and the laughter we connected the past
to the present and future and long may they last
And if time could be measured in love and not years
and laughter be tonic to vanish the fears
we can say we have captured the secret of living
and are ready to tackle the next step that's given

my first communion

on a maiden voyage sailed to an island roamed the hillsides
sat by the ocean . . . it was nice
wandered through town shopped for trinkets exercised
     muscles
slept without deadline . . . it was nice
dealt out guilt passed by discomfort explored the need
this solitary traveller . . . it was nice
searched for self scribbled some verse zoomed into camera
read through the night . . . it was very nice

"go to Duck Creek" landlady suggested "it's half-hour away"
"sure thing, why not" car parked across road
backpack strapped on extra runners bottle of water
no camera bought wrong film map ready at entrance
typical hiking path must be cooler than 35 degrees
inside those trees eager for nature no other person there
striding onto pathway entered eternity invisible tiptoes
shifted the steps earthlife took over no person was left

stepping deep into the throbbing veins of my eternal spirit
I touch the living voice of Mother Nature's tenderness
and yield to sunlit velvet flavours of her emerald scent
evaporating into that nourishing heavenly kingdom
which is firmly rooted in the bountiful majesty of Earth
we are one heartbeat she and I today this moment
one pure melody whispers through our stream-lapped foliage
tiptoeing in hushes of new shooting stems in buried logs
worshipped sound connecting neon mosses stump to stump
with timbered kaleidoscopic branching leaves in sky
rolling in harmony to the holy wisdom in each whetted stone
we are one song she and I today this moment

returned next morning confirmation of space visible beauty
and camera with film . . . it was nice
smiled at tourists shared old growth trees artistic inspired
words in our eyes . . . it was nice
mind at networking sealing the scenes nature perfection
each step an old friend . . . it was nice
nowhere eternal communion was gone yet my moment's mine
transformation done . . . it was consummate

Cottonwood Treasurehouse

Winking at the wind
Laughing lilting leaves
Dancing round my world
Fingers of the trees

Fanciful and free
Braver than the breeze
Nature at its best
Catch me if you please

Childhood enhanced
Inside a treehouse rink
But sparkling eyes retreat
In disappearing ink

a fight to the finish

this Doukhobor baby girl
born a "prairie chicken" with the train whistle in her ears
riding to span two families
arrived kicking and screaming
legs baptised in blue blood
stubborn head appearing last
"bassackward baby" her brother teased
elongated frustrated not quite emancipated
woman to be sister seven years later
woman hating cleaning and cooking
convention
hating the hating
kicking and screaming through fifty years
of babies and family and singing and travelling
cooking and cleaning and canning
and rational planning
fighting fatalism lethargy trying to fit in
not giving in
spending bank's money and teaching and learning
forever returning to the vision within
her ancestral family
Russian language culture
martyrdom wisdom of elders growing
timeless weight beyond knowing
vision with logic illogically yearning
without a need so immersed in love
without a need to need so much
talking too much and saying too little
lonely forever inside her head
finding reading and writing instead
never an end in sight
surface contorted distorted
yet so well promoted against the grain
stubborn belief

inside a community of ideal hearts
fed and feeding mouthfuls of soul and conscience
commitment responsibility
a heavy load to carry
from embryonic beginnings
birthplaces of blood flow an ocean away
vitamins minerals good health
saranwrapped in a womb of protection
constant inspection
racing to excel to be equal
opportunities past discrimination
integration
please no assimilation
just keep altering the outside to fit in the holes
holes become goals
and society shrinks
weak links erase the connections
deception to truths impossible to hide
labouring to breathe
labouring to live
labouring to nurture a vision
evolution against the grain
vegetarian swallowing
wallowing in everything whole
undigested perfection twisting
heaven on earth
eternally hungry for peace of mind
frustrated not quite emancipated
this bassackward baby
suddenly a popular minority
woman in the world
in the community
Doukhobor
ethnic distinction must not have extinction
open negotiations to wisdom in souls
children revive the light with their eyes

faith again lifts the banner high
safely incubated perpetuated
brothers sisters soulmates children
forever children
to see consummation
their happiness grown
whatever was sown should almost be done
there must be a final run
a fight to the finish
designed for a gift to the future
we ride on our train
Doukhobors full
watching scorched fields
swollen bodies
bloodstained dew
breathing foul air
and praying
praying for harvests in their true places
believing and living
still suspended through time
eternal consciousness
invincible Doukhobor essence
forever real
toil and peaceful life
a global village
an equal reality for everyone
it's a fight to the finish
rich soil growing
must be growing
bountiful crops of children and laughter
truth full to eat ever after
then finally
finally
comes the rest
peaceful at last
this Doukhobor baby girl

ferry watch

hiding in sunglasses sunburned in fear
ads for frustration in handbags of tears
boasting of t-shirts in razor-sharp screams
tasting of coffee with succulent dreams
scented by armpits of christian dior
wearing loud laughter with gold to the floor
sharing their wrinkles through brown muscletones
dangling their children from dieted bones
pictures of mouthwash in dreadlocked size
whistling nostrils and spandex thighs
armed with newspapers in designer clothes
filled by pepsi in stunted growths
feeling like velvet in coloured smiles
sailing on snores to the next green isle

sisters

women
are bonded
in sisterhood

a flash of light
insight
together shared
we're in the hood
sisterhood

there are sisters
through blood
and kin
my sister
her sister
is me
sisterhood

there are sisters
and sisters
but my sister
stays
that sister
who moves me
I stay
to the good
sisterhood

life bonds us
like minds us
commitment
true grit
evolvement
involvement

we keep all our wit
together
foul weather
some choices are free
compassions
we stash 'em
we long to agree
yet sounding
we go on
loving understood

us sisters
are bonded
for all sisterhood

Character

Thick, Thin
Out, In
Gnarled, Bandaged
Fresh or Green

Hairy, Callous
Corny, Cropped
Manufactured
At a drop

Lithe or Porous
Brittle-boned
Leaning forward
Close to home

Does it ever
stand alone?

The Eyes Have It

I used to draw
the eye
over and over and over again
I used to spend
hours
trying to understand
the
meaning
of
a
man
by drawing
the eye
over and over and over again
the left eye
the right eye
the old eye
the bright eye
in committed detail
in unswerving dedication
in the
need
to discover
the naked Truth
of
a
man

and then
I looked
into
two eyes

Perception

I see the outline
In black and white
The wrinkles
The crinkles
The dimples
They light.
The outsider's sight.

But the stuff within
Where someone's been
The churnings
The burnings
The yearnings
They dim.
It's not in my ken.

Gossip

Cluck, cluck
Cluck, cluck
What can I today upchuck

Surely it's the worst to be
Clucking up another's tree?

A Metaphor

A person begins as
    a subject a noun
    that is seen at first
    in a simple sound
    then describing words
    all gather around
Soon a person becomes
    an action a verb
    that is forming direction
    a subject disturbed
    with adverbs and motion
    as yet of unheard
A person will grow to
    a colour described
    personification
    in a run-on size
    with prepositions
    and future tense emphasized
A person may jump to
    a complex clause
    that's a transitive thought
    connecting across
    with different conjunctions
    giving it pause
Or a person could be
    just a simple phrase
    that's identified split
    in a succinct phase
    a kind of aspect
    in its predicated case
A person may rise to
    a full-blown sentence
    that is modified dangled
    colloquially dense

still yet incompleted
but making some sense
Then a person ends as
a direct object a word
that is passive inverted
abstracted observed
compounded now simple
an article blurred

Crosswinds of Character

Hearts thunder
releasing
unbridled Passion
kicking and screaming

Brains dictate
producing
clearcut Logic
with calm consistency

Passion pounces on life
gobbling voraciously
through
indiscriminate bites

Logic launders life
chewing languidly
at
particular rights

Logic and Passion
tossed
into
the same boat
produce
a curious
load—
thunder and lightning
calm sea ahead
tidal wave
safe waterbed

Would that neither in us e'er be dead!

To My Daughter Sarah

Your face
Its grace
Smiles sunshine
Every place

Your hair
Its flair
Cascading
Every where

Your eyes
A prize
Dance soulful
No disguise

Your voice
The choice
A nightingale
Employs

Your heart
Imparts
Love Goodness
God's mark

The years
Bring tears
Childhood echoes
Disappear

The Meaning of Being a Mom

I never thought I'd be a Mom
It was God's gift not for everyone
And then they came, one, two, and three
It was then I learned my destiny
They taught me more than books had done
Starting from our eldest son
He was quiet and happy and patient and smart
One of those babies who steals everyone's heart
And then our next son was born so wise
Tears and laughter shone free in his honest eyes
Our daughter came last as the crowning glory
She shyly said little but told the whole story
And borne along with them were their many friends
Their cousins their soul mates—a mom's love never ends.

Now when I'm shrivelled inside my dark places
The children appear and I'm warmed in their graces
I'm lifted and filled up at once to the soul
When I see all the love and the hope they bestow
Moms must have a part in them roaming about
An unidentified organ near the stomach or heart
It hurts and it bears and it twists and it turns
And it gives and receives yet one never learns
What exactly "it" is, that bottomless well
Is it blood vein or muscle or tissue or cell
That continues to breed a belief in the Good
To work and to care, to forgive as we should
Because
    our children
       would.

An Ode to Us

There's still some hope
even if we're fat
when we've got wisdom
cuddling in our lap

We can watch
our children grow
We can smile
for we smugly know

They'll grow up
in turn to breed
a race of thinkers
with an awesome creed

"Toil and Peaceful Life"
—Yes, there is reason to survive!—
Our future must mean
Fat mothers with a dream!

to dad

choir voices singing
years ago
in Saskatchewan
when you were leaving
on a freight train
to your future

men forever question
if a tree falls in the forest
and no one hears
does it make a sound

then if people sang
over fifty years ago
and we never heard them
were the songs really sung

it's like the bird
flying into the clouds
is it still there
if the eye doesn't see it

they say our people lived
by what they believed
over a century ago
but we didn't see them

today I understand
when I look into my children's eyes
and see reflected
the lives of their ancestors
my ancestors
I understand
that everything is real

what was given to you
has been given to us
will be given to future generations
and whether we are present
to hear and to see and to live it
does not determine the truth
of the essence
that was, is, and will be

you taught us that

choir voices singing
today
in Grand Forks
when you are arriving
with your future

Eulogy to Eileen

When I woke up to life
She was waking up too
We saw the same sun
And we smiled at the dew
When I went to school
She was walking there too
We read the same books
And we learned and we grew
We were neighbours as kids
And we shared the same street
But inside her and me
The same heart did not beat
She was better somehow
Honest, fair, good to all
She was one of a kind
Above others, stood tall
And her laughter rang free
As each year she did trace
A true love of life
Shone on her smiling face
What I never could catch
Was how she knew the score
Where life's meaning was at
And what it had in store
She carried some map
In her heart, in her soul
That taught her to love
To accept her tough role
I was her neighbour
But she was my friend
And I will always remember
Though the years are all spent
Now today as we part
And Eileen goes elsewhere

I would like to give thanks
For the childhood she shared
I know at her new place
In eternity too
She's already a friend
And her laughter rings true

My Parents

Yesterday when I was young
Parents were something that tagged along
    into my personal places
    and fragile spaces
      uninvited.
Yesterday when I was a child
Parents I believed were out of style
    with concerned faces
    spouting outdated graces
      uninterrupted.
Yesterday when I was a youth
I sadly treaded a familiar route
    of climbing the fence
    into a pool of offence
      against parents.

But that was yesterday, and yesterday's gone.

Today when I grew older
And the pool that I sat in considerably colder
    I glanced over to see
    my parents waiting for me
      unwavering.
Today when I've grown tired
There are my parents still not retired
    their hearts tuned to song
    with wise counsel along
      supporting.

But that is today, and today's almost gone.

Tomorrow I woke in a paralyzed fear
My parents had vanished in a nightmarish tear
　　I screamed out in fright
　　they had gone in the night
　　　forevermore.

So today's the day that's vital you see
Today I can tell them, my parents, quickly
　　how patient how kind
　　what models I find
　　　in my parents
　　how loving how wise
　　what a perfect size
　　　are my parents.
There is nothing on earth or in heaven can be
Nothing nobler or greater or wiser for me
　　with their concerned faces
　　and their precious graces
　　　than my parents.

To My Mother

We are attached we three
She and you and me
It doesn't matter what I say or do
The mirror's image shines right through

From you my revered mother to my revered daughter

Connecting ancient rhythms through each girlhood eyes
Bearing the tears of our unique history's sacrifice
Woman fostering the will of being strong
Spiritual searching for the next touch to belong
Arms crossed across each mother's chest

Hands stretched forth to every other hand
Bound by our destiny across all global land
The umbilical cord pulls together endless time
I'm blessed to share in something that's not mine

Eternal human roots that join eternal lines

Through you to me to she
Us three
Reverently

Interesting . . .

When I write about my loved ones
I write mostly in rhyme
Must be the heartbeat that I live
That's made in perfect time

But when I begin to grope through words to search for
the essential ingredient of life
to explore or justify or change or comment on the
direction humankind seems to be taking
I find no rhyme
I wonder, will there be, some time?

The Quantum Quest

wandering yearning groping
wearied anguished parched
alone
analyzing reading writing
confused impassioned driven
alone

      inquiring discussing singing
      strengthened hopeful excited
      together
      working sharing loving
      nourished balanced connected
      together

Folly

At my urgent grasp's mark
My taut digits' extreme
Swings—the pendulum's heart

One herculean strain more
One last strenuous spread
And—the gorged plummet's core

But alas once again
The prize slips into naught
As—the stretch proves in vain

Relish frothing its seams
Truth eluding the grasp
Life—still dangles extremes

Without wit, without wit

Options or Not, That Is the Question

this\that

rocky\flat · thin\fat

go\stay · then\now

work\play · · · · · · · · · · · · · · · · · write\plough

short\long · · · · · · · · · · · · · · · shallow\deep

weak\strong · · · · · · · · · · · · · · · · · sow\reap

share\own · we\me

talk\moan · · · · · · · · · · · · · · · · · · cost\free

laugh\cry · · · · · · · · · · · · · · · silver\gold

live\die · · · · · · · · · · · · · · · · · young\old

choice\fate · · · · · · · · · · early\late

love\hate

What was it Shakespeare said . . .

Was it that NOW in time
is just a forming memory
that grew
into a future
looking back at NOW?

Will it be THEN
the true
reality of where
in NOW
we live

. . . and HOW?

being used

is useful
only
if
the user
is
also
being used

last moments in great-grandmother's life

fragile spider thread
still suspending death

feeble echoes sound
heartbeat fading down

sighs within each sleep
beckoning for peace

sum of life dissolved
mysteries unsolved

On Death

Will I whimper shiver
Beg journey's end?
Will I screaming fight
Life's last gasp to defend?

Will I fold up my arms
Lie down in defeat?
Will I help Fate along
Death run eager to greet?

Will I go "placidly"
Without a "moan"?
Will I "bearing the brunt"
Stay strong to the bone?

Will whatever I do
When the unknown beckons,
Will whatever it be
There shall be no seconds.

Western Philosophy I

Age is free
as is destiny
Life is fine
if you tow the line
Pay for the gritz
and stay at the Ritz
Forget the poor boy
be selfish, enjoy
For age is free
as is destiny

Each day is yours
who cares for the whores
No worry or sweat
it ain't your time yet
Pucker up and explore
don't be such a bore
For age is free
as is destiny

Sewers are made
in the lowest grade
And paupers are gone
before too long
So what's it to me
I'm not paying the fee
For age is free
as is destiny

You're there I'm here
so what do I care
'Twas the toss of the sperm
that determined my term
I'm here for the fun
I'll be seeing you, hon
For age is free
. . . and my destiny?

Western Philosophy II

Pearls and diamonds
and silver and gold
These are the riches
by which to grow old
Who cares about lovin'
and sharin' and trust
We all know they soon
become rusted to dust

Money and power and
good looks to flaunt
Let's be honest here, mister
nothin's left then to want
Good nature and wisdom
and honesty's fine
But not when you've bought
our American line

Okay fine I've got it
and I've learned the rhyme
But I'm not yet happy
so what's been my crime
I've done all the "right" things
I've thrown out the grey
But peace still eludes me
so what now?—to pray!

Yes, church is the answer
with just once a week
On Sundays I'll save me
I'll not be a freak
I don't want to carry
the burden to grow
Just give me fast answers
like Billy Graham's show

Okay fine I've got it
and I've done the time
But yet I'm not happy
so now what's my crime
. . . Oh, God, surely Thou Art
not going to say
I must live my life
to my conscience each day

That's a whole new concept
I'd rather not face
To see and to carry
to understand. Oh, erase!
Now you've really gone done it
and I'm in a mess
because life's turned right over
. . . on my lap I guess . . .

apathy

careless
I feel careless
about life

precious
what's so precious
about life

things come
things go
we buy
we store
we lock the door

there's nothing more

the collector

backpacking claustrophobia in the Ancient Medina
railroading enigmas from homeland Siberia
tracing inspiration through historical *rues*
camelling the peace of Saharid's dunes
shipping out ocean bottles of echoing sun
inhaling some green before the rainforest's done
hiking up bruised volcanoes unmarked by man
swallowing clouds whole in a metal wingspan
    gentle succour through guarded sigh
    fatal piercing with soul-filled eye
    grimaced gestures in connecting tongue
    smiling and hugging till all is sung
    bargained and tasted and bought and brought
    stolen hearts visions pots rum and what not
    velvet ideas words moments and rings
    taking what's mine from each newfound thing
searching out gathering collecting by heart
of things and of people each precious fresh part
the bits and the pieces my ingredients all
I'm adding essentials to make me stand tall
scurrying and hurrying to add to the form
must pick up new findings then rush and go home
to finish the full to fill up all the whole
to piece it together from headtop to sole
    yet they're just bits and pieces
    strewn surface to core
    collector collecting collecting
    some more . . .

Our Daily Life

Each latest millisecond
Of our immediate present
slips
through the neck
of life's hourglass,
linking
the diminishing past
to the expanding future
one millisecond
at
a
time.

Each one millisecond
which passes by
in a millisecond
is our Daily Life.

A Mother's Daily Life

In this individual
woman's physical self
breathes
a spirit of life
passing
through the pores
of the hourglass anatomy,
linking
the head of the love
to the heart of embryo
which grows into
that new being
who delivers
her from
the diminishing past
into the
expanding future.

Each one embryo
which passes through
in a millisecond
provides a mother with
her Daily Life.

Respiratory System

Pores feel
the scent
Inhale
and bend

Absorbed
descend
They nestle
spent

Exude
expend
Then lift
extend

Pores fill
with scent
Inhaled
they end

Horse's Goals

"Horses with blinders on are good,"
my dad could see I had not understood.

"They plod on ahead without any distraction,"
he repeated again but with no satisfaction.

"But they miss seeing the panoramic view,"
I continued to argue the right thing to do.

"Let's remove the confining blinders please,
you'll see they'll be better off without these."

"They'll stay in one place just twirling around
and my cornfield this way will never get ploughed."

My dad would shake his head and sigh,
I grew up in the echo of my last try.

Now I'm tired of twirling around and around
and I think I am ready to put blinders on.

Sometime

There'll be a time
within my life
When things
        will change
I do not mind

I wait
I try to find
the meaning.

There'll be a time
within my life
When things
        will change
It is destined.

I wait
I try to find
the patience.

The Muse

I was content until that curs'ed Fate it interfered
And introduced a man into whose eyes I disappeared
He held me tightly from across a vacuum space
And till this moment I cannot forget his face

Without an outstretched hand he handed me a prize
It was my naked self without the least disguise
Yet I in turn replied with just the barest smile
Afraid afraid to death to open up the raging fire

But as I sink into the once familiar drain
I hear the ever-hollowing echo of my name
And somewhere deep inside I feel a newborne beating
It is relentless and it will not take defeating

The Youth of Old Age

When we were children
Anything was possible
Life was a rubber ball we could carelessly toss
Near one time and then lightheartedly far
Never fearing a miss or a drop or a loss
Of that precious ball

When we were teenagers
Very little was possible
Life was a glass ball we shakingly held
In a tightwire act
Afraid of a fall and a crashing
Of that precious ball

When we were young parents
Some things were possible
Life was a crystal ball of exciting visions
With past and future in the present
Worrying about bringing up
Being brought up and enjoying it all

Suddenly it's here:
The Youth of Old Age
The time between parenting and grandparenting
The time of a breath for oneself
The time of embracing life when again
Many things are possible

Yes, life is a ball
A global ball
In which we are participants
In which we can create as we choose
In which we are connected
And anything is possible

The Youth of Old Age
The best time of life so far!

lying on a beach in Venezuela, reading a magazine, while local poor people circle around us basking foreigners

I think . . .
> I'm questioning my maniacal need to see
> I'm wondering what the meaning of this life's to be . . .

I read . . .
> A photojournalist sits in revolution's eye
> Exposing what? Or just another lemming's wish to die?

I see . . .
> She photographs an "idealistic" freedom's fight
> That's riddled with a death-infested "right."

I watch . . .
> The masses hyperventilate beneath the rich man's feet
> Shedding their priceless goodness for a chance to use his
> seat.

I think . . .
> I'm questioning how much more there is to see
> I'm wondering what the meaning of this life's for me . . .

Nostalgia

. . . Twenty years of idealism down the drain—
From youthful optimism to mid-life strain . . .

    Where did all the good times go?
    How did we become part of the middle-class flow
    When we were so sure we knew what we were doing
    And always felt our future was ahead?
    We thought we'd always keep the '60's thinking going
    Yet laid it on the dormant shelf instead!
    —And now just look where "normal" life has led:
    Right into the mundane pot we've spread!
    For dollars and houses and cars and children,
    We've pushed and we've shoved 'round and 'round in the
    cauldron.
    "Work harder, run faster, try everything new!"
    "Be better and watch your report cards too!"
    —We've become embroiled in North America's stew!
    Buying ten-minute happiness in neon stores,
    Sharing empty dark eyes each with each more and more.
    —For, when a drop of reality hits us,
    We smudge it real quick to see only what fits us.
    "Don't stop, don't think, don't quit the racin'
    'Cause you just may see the future you're facin'!"

. . . Twenty years of idealism down the drain—
From youth full aspirations to mid-life pain . . .

Are we too late to turn the tide?
Can we yet stop and look inside?
Have we still got some spirit and drive
To set our course for our souls to survive,
To give our children a world alive
With passion and feeling for beliefs to strive
In a fresh space in which their children can thrive?

. . . Twenty years of idealism . . . down the drain?
Or has it survived for mid-life to reclaim? . . .

I Wish

to find the space
    of my beginning
to breathe the air
    from which I sprang
to feel the place
    within my spirit
and stand there, naked, fearless, strong

I NEED

to shed the cloak
    of glutted fabric
to rid the days
    of wasted time
to crush the seed
    of bane ambition
and move ahead new, weightless, strong

The Think-and-Do Book

I think
I look
I write
A book

It seems
To me
To set
Me free

yet as I sit
and stare outside
I see to think
is just to hide

I must
I can
I will
I plan

To jump
In to
The fray—
To Do!

No second thoughts
No turning back
No time to waste
It's NOT too late

Doggerel
Et Al

Redundancy, I see you smile
  Redundantly!
Redundancy, You are in fact
  My fact of life!

The Recipe for Letting Your Imagination Run Away with You

Take one flabby sock of a mind and
Pop in a drop of an idea
Laced with
A pinch of a possibility and
If the timing is ripe with hope
Sometimes
It rises into
A fantastical expanse of inspiration that
Lifts you with ecstasy
Ever-swelling until
It explodes into
A downpour of melting visions
Leaving behind
A deflated sock of a mind

biding our time

let's kiss and make up
since there's time to kill
let's forget
the setup
and head for the hills
the frills are frilling
the rest's left to God
let's forget
the setup
and head where it's hot
we'll kiss and make up
till the station is filled
with fuel for turning
life
round to within
we'll be back
for the answers
complete
ready to trill
to fill up souls' fires
we'll then swallow
the pill
but till then
please
let's make up and
head for those hills

Battlecry of Our People

I look to my left
I look to my right
I see all around me
A most breathtaking sight

Sisters have gathered
Our brothers have too
We're standing together
We're out in full view

We're walking on forward
With shoulder to shoulder
The Future has beckoned
It renders us bolder

Whatever will greet us
As we shed our old ways
As we step off the treadmill
We know we can face

With Faith for foundation
And Love in our soul
With Reason and Conscience
and Will—to our goal!

Fun with Physiognomy

It can't be just at random
that two arms hang by our sides
that our elbows turn sharp corners
that our fingers spread so wide

It can't just be at random
that our hands move north and south
to scratch the spot that itches
to stuff food in our mouth

It just can't be at random
that we're made the way we are
with legs that move and guide us
on soles (souls, ha!) to take us far

No! There's got to be some method
to the make-up of our bods (yuk!)
Some method though eludes us
yet alludes to greater odds—(gods?)

Coffee

Oh, what a thrill
To drink its fill
From those two Hills
. . . Brothers that is . . .

It heats me still
And will until
I get the bill
. . . health that is . . .

Camping

. . . and we set up
and we sit down
sweat is pouring
This is camping

. . . and the friends come
and we eat more
there is singing
This is camping

. . . and the sun's hot
and the lake's cool
we're all basking
This is camping

. . . and there's laughter
and discussions
glasses clinking
This is camping

. . . and the stars shine
and the fire burns
seedshells spitting
This is camping

. . . and the rain falls
and there's puddles
we're all hiding
This is camping

... and the time's shared
and the hugs made
we're all packing
This was camping

I love camping

The Joy of Travelling

Please let me on the bus, dude
Get me on a train
Set me down and
Drive away again
    'Tis best you understand, son
    The ship is in for me
    Set me down and
    Sail away to sea
Jet me to the isle, man
Rocket to the moon
Set me down and
Get me there by noon
    There's nothing left out here, mate
    But space can get me far
    So set me down and
    Reach out to a star
Hey what's the problem now, sir
Your pathway seems too long
Just jump astride my travelbug
We'll journey for a song
    Come one come all I beckon you
    Let's swim the waves together
    There's room to go inside my show
    We'll ride through life forever

Stagnant Doggerel\Failing Old Guard

Who's in the know?
How does it go?
Where does it say
It has to stay?
... Whoever started it that way? ...

How do we grow?
Where can we go?
Why do we pray
To save the day?
... When there is hardship in decay? ...

We're here to show
There's pain in tow
When some folks stay
The same old way!
... Whyever do we have to pay? ...

How easy can we love today
How easy to our children say
Go find a way to change the day
And we will help you on your way
And see a future come what may
We must speed up without delay
Or we will with our spirits pay

And if I rhyme some more this way
I will become too old and grey
Those children will no more obey
But bring me food upon a tray
So I will stop no more to play
And if you want just press replay
And if you don't go make some hay
            okay?
                good day!

Sillification

Get better quick, Taresa—

Sometimes some seemingly sane souls stretch sanity
somewhat, slipping slightly into singularly symbolic spaces.
So since sunrise, some scribing souls smilingly
schemed—successfully?—to speed some sincerely-special
signs of support straight to someone special sitting, straining,
sleeping, struggling, scrambling, to secure some sufficiently
solid salubrity.

Sincerely, Stephen's silly senior citizens and siblings

Happy birthday, Olga—

To think time ticked tirelessly towards today through
tantalizing trips to tell tales of two (times two) travellers
treading toward tomorrow's truths. Take time to think, to
temper things, to taste time tenderly. Toast time! The tape
touches traditional tumultuous thoughts.
The true tutor trying till time tells

Salutations, Daniel & Holly—

Sitting still certainly solidifies spiritual sanity sometimes,
since ceaseless speeding significantly stifles spirit stimuli.
Still, students striving, stubbornly struggling, stand soulfully
sublime, since circumstances surrounding studying simply
slander society's solidarity. Socrates stated social skills sink
since psychology supercedes strenuous stretches. So, sitting
and strength stimulation saves success, some soccer, surfing,
skydiving, serious saxophoning, singing, sneezing . . . smile.

Sincerely, serial sequence seven sender

Rhyming Couplets for a Rhyming Couple

Picture: The Lion's Gate Bridge at Night

Our anniversary marks
A time in my heart
When life for me grew
And connected us two
forever

Through schooling and time
Through babies and rhyme
In Victoria and Van.
Our life with you ran
unpredictably

And now that we're here
In our twenty-fifth year
I thought that I'd share
A reminder of where
we began

Every time that you glance
At this print by perchance
May it bring you a smile
Remembering our miles
together

And may it serve as a sign
Of our love for all time
The bridge that shines bright
And joins through the nights
you and me

Epilogue

In Retrospect

I have to confess
I have no sadnéss
    I treasure the minutes

Despite the unrest
The long endless quest
    I treasure the minutes

If I had to begin
To do it again
I'd do it the same
Choose the way that I came
    I treasure the minutes

My only regret
Is I have a good bet
That the road which I set
Left me greatly in debt
    To my loved ones

They lived their life true
As I fretted and drew
My insides in hue
Of colours for view
    And I love them
        Forever
            Thank yóu

Afterword

I have deliberated over publishing these poems partly because there is such a wide range of sophistication in them. However, much as I have tried to extricate the poor from the polished, I could not. Somehow, each continues to hold its unique, necessary place in my literary repertoire that has been compiled over the last thirty years, just as each student has had his/her unique, necessary place in my school family over those same thirty years. The dramatic range in their academic abilities did not change my level of commitment to them as contributing individuals in our world. Each poem contributes to my world.

The other reason for my procrastination is related to the first. Each time I think I am reaching the decision to publish, I get an overwhelming feeling of sadness and loss on behalf of those poems that may yet be written, but will not make it into this collection. As a result, I have continued waiting for one more moment in time, my time, to be captured in words before final printing. This time I've done it. My apologies to any future words and verses that are lying in my subconscious, as of yet unborn.